THE GREAT McGONAGALL SCRAP BOOK

Ladies and gentlemen
from the book of the film
we give you the life of McGonagall
through his press cuttings–
talks, bubbles and suit lengths.
–every word in this book
is genuine and has no artificial
colouring matter except for
'isanythingwornunderthekilt'.

THE GREAT McGONAGALL SCRAP BOOK

by
Spike Milligan
and
Jack Hobbs

A STAR BOOK
published by
WYNDHAM PUBLICATIONS

TO

SIR WILLIAM TOPAZ MCGONAGALL

POET

A STAR BOOK

Published in 1976 by
WYNDHAM PUBLICATIONS LTD
A Howard & Wyndham Company
123 King Street, London W6 9JG

First published in Great Britain by
M & J Hobbs in association with
Michael Joseph Ltd, 1975

The publishers wish to thank David Winter & Son for permission to reproduce some McGonagall Poems which originally appeared in POETIC GEMS

ISBN 0352 39778 0

Printed by Hazells Offset Ltd.
Leigh Road, Slough, Berks.

The Film
THE GREAT McGONAGALL

Features

SPIKE MILLIGAN
PETER SELLERS
JULIA FOSTER
JOHN BLUTHAL

VALENTINE DYALL
CLIFTON JONES
JULIAN CHAGRIN
VICTOR SPINETTI
CHARLIE ATOM

Screenplay by JOSEPH McGRATH
SPIKE MILLIGAN

Produced by DAVID GRANT

Directed by JOSEPH McGRATH

A DARLTON PRODUCTION
released through
TIGON FILM DISTRIBUTORS LTD

CLAP!
CLAP!
CLAP!
It's not real clapping you know
—they put these talks
bubbles on afterwards
—in fact I haven't said a word.
CLAP!

CLAP!

CLAP!

AP!

CLAP!

CLAP!

The Rev. George Gilfillan

In 1840 I was approached by a Scottish man wearing a kilt under which nothing was worn, who asked me

a) who he was.

I told him according to the accounts at the Army and Navy Stores, Greenock, he was William McGonagall the well-known overdraft and trainee Massage Parlour. "William McGonegall?" he echoed "That's an ideal name for the stage." So I put him on the next Wells Fargo and we named the stage 'The Wells Fargo Massage Parlour.'

"You've given me a great start" he shouted, "Boo" I screamed and gave him another one (1). Then I cried "On your marks, get set, go" and away he went on a new career - in fact he careered across the road straight into a bus. "I want you to become my theatrical agent and run alongside this stage until I get my first engagement" he said, whereupon he slid a ring over his third finger and cried "This is my first engagement." It took him half an hour to sing it.

And so a great bond was struck up and later struck down as was McGonagall many times. In this book I have opened my archives and was subsequently arrested for indecent exposure. I allowed the publisher access to these rare press cuttings (that is there were only two of them). However by revamping them several times we have managed to get a substantial book which you now hold in your hand. It shows the triumph of McGonagall over adversity but also shows the triumph of adversity over McGonagall. He was three down and one to go when last heard of.

His long, arduous and painful career spans a decayed. And he will always be remembered by his witty catch phrase:-

"Will you please stop throwing those rotten vegetables at me!"

Signed.

The Reverend George Gilfillan

Cell Block 3,

Wormwood Scrubs

(Key under mat).

If I hide my left hand I'll get it in without paying duty on it.

Ladies will be pleased to know that an evening of free entertainment will be given in the laundry room on the evening of April the First.

The programme will start at 6 p.m. and end at midnight.

It will consist of three Shakespearian plays adapted into the Scottish by an unknown assailant.

They will be Hamlet Part I, Edward IV Part II, and the entire three acts of Othello. The cast is as follows :-

William McGonagall (Quick Change Artist)

who has promised not to have a silver collection unless overcome by hunger.

We attach his letter of introduction.

Mary Stewart-Fugg

Signed -

Mary Stewart-Fugg, Superior

May 3rd 1838

We have examined the drains underneath Mr. McGonagall
and have found them to be in a reasonable condition.
There is a waste pipe which carries away the
effluviant to a height of ten feet.
In the light of all these findings we see no
reason why he should not continue to give
his renderings of Shakespeare over any of
the Sewerage systems of the district.
We would warn however that this could change at any minute.

Your most obedient servant at all times,

James MacToley,
Chief Sanitary Inspector.

P.S. Mr. Blakethorpe-Scrowl is away on holiday.

Bed 3
Dumfries YMCA
3 of Snal 1839

Ma dear Madam.

It just sae harpoons that I ha fallen vacant on the nicht of Apri the first and with gud will cered be extended tae June the 3rd. During this period I am willing tae put on some gems of Thespianism for the combined inclusive fee of 'one hot dinner' (hereafter known as The food) The whole of ma act is pure and liscenced by the Dundee department of Sanitation and Agriculture, I have three certificates guranteeing me free from foul peet and swine fever. Im sure that the washers, ironers and scrubbers will be much improved and releived by ma manly bearings and the power of my high nasal voice, and I am willing tae sing melodies on request or sooner. I woud appreciate if nae ~~alcohol~~ alcohol or fruit were consumed during ma performance, and can aw empty bottles be hidden, along with sticks, clubs, blackjacks etc. A word of caution: I have been known tae tak wi a seizure upon opening envelopes and finding nay money inside, as a precaution

I must ask & ye tae enclose a powerful ten shilling nate as near the top o the envelope as possible -

Yrrrrs faithfuccy

William J McGonagall

Retired unemployed weaver and Thespian

Ps I must be assured of safe passage twn Stage and dressing rame

McGonagall having a seizure after opening an envelope with nae money in it.

Och Nagger mah fair i the nicknummoch by the killicaddi macrea macopologies the noo!

I'm up here now Daddy
You swine—you'll be hearing from my solicitor in the morning.
That's funny—you don't look Jewish!

The Dumfries Laundry
and District News

Last Sunday night in the absence of any entertainment in the district, an unusual presentation of Shakespeare to the Laundry Ladies at the Women's Institute for Sailors' Wives took place. The setting of the stage was unique and showed a tendency towards the new modernism, that is ten planks on top of six beer barrels (one leaking) represented the Palace at Elsinore. Some clothes line on which sheets were drying was used as curtains. There was no illumination except for the cast holding his own candle.

The entire show, to my surprise, was done by one William McGonagall who assured the ladies at the start that 'Nothing was worn under the kilt'. He chose a brilliant moment to reveal this – that is, half way through the Hamlet soliloquy – once again showing this man's tremendous trend towards the new liberalism in the theatre. The raising of the kilt and the pointing at the codpiece were also well received by the ladies, some of whom were overcome and carried out but insisted on being carried in again for the encore, when there was some trouble caused by the positioning of his candle, which caused some burning round the edges. He seemed to recover from this however and unfortunately continued his performance. The energy he generated was unbelievable. It became a bit tiresome when he had to rush off and change into Ophelia coming on to say 'What ails thee my lord?' then rush off, reappear as Hamlet and say 'Pardon?' then exit and reappear as Ophelia again. It was during this tender duologue that he again restated that 'Nothing was worn under the kilt', being careful the while over the positioning of the candle. It was a unique moment in the history of the Laundryroom when at the conclusion of the soliloquy he rushed forward and shouted 'Altogether now' pointing at a chart of the words. I did not wait until the end of the performance but I would say that William McGonagall will go a long way. He will not get better of course, but he'll go a long way. He'll have to. He daren't stay long in one place.

JAMES AGATE.

Lady washerman overcome – weeping after the McGonagall codpiece incident.

McGonagall exposing the second half of his act to the washerwoman.

McGonagall's laundry list during the week of
the Shakespearian Festival Isle of Mull Working Mens Club

1 VEST (Unclaimed)

Variety Weekly

New York, May 1838

McGONAGALL BOFFO AT WOMENS INSTITUTE, SCOT ROCKS WASHERS, BARD BURNS BALLS,

Last night a stage door Johnny mobbed William T McGonagall after his performance. He approached him and said "Sir you are a Scottish patriot and literary giant. Do you like Burns?' 'Aye' said McGonagall. 'Then cop this' said the man and stuck a red hot poker up his kilt. The police took him into custody but later after paying ten punds bail, McGonagall was released.

However the evening had been a theatrical triumph for the audience who were models of restraint. The models were later sold to a lady of Rank. A Miss Sylvia Xerox.

NEXT WEEK McGONAGALL LIVE AT LEWISHAM TOWN HALL – ADMISSION FREE EXCEPT FOR McGONAGALL – B.U.P.

Bought of
Doctor Angus Muckreekie,
The Tassells,
3, Crummock up the flae,
Dingles

To attending the thespian William T. McGonagall
at his country bus stop.
First degree burns to Scrotum
To applying sparrows teeth poultice,
setting on of one hundred leeches.
Followed by immediate treatment for anaemia.
.... 3 guineas

NOTE:

On his deathbed McGonagall related the story of the bill to me. After the death of the leeches from blood poisoning, McGonagall demanded to know the nature of his disease. "It's Alpinial Dandruff from a great height." said the physician. "I demand a second opinion" said McGonegall. "Right I'll give it to you" said the doctor, "it's Alpinial Dandruff, and that will cost you another 3 guineas." "I heard you the first time" said McGonagall.

I being of sound mind do hereby declare this statement to be true.

signed

The Reverend George Gilfillan
Home for Insane Vicars

P.S. I love you
P.P.S That'll be 3 guineas.

The Times In The Courts May 1848

Before Justice Mr. Rotten-Thudd a vagrant actor giving his name as Sir Stafford Cripps was charged with loitering at a bus stop with intent to eat. When asked what excuse he had to offer he said "I was on my way back". The constable said he had cautioned him with his truncheon twice to no effect except for a small change in the outline of his head. When asked by the judge "Was anything worn under the kilt?" he replied "No, just badly burnt". He then sang 'Bonnie Mary of Argyll' and was sentenced to fourteen days in a cell with Bonnie Mary herself who was really a retired Admiral of the Fleet/Nun who was serving time for doing a full frontal in the face of the advancing enemy.

Why do you keep on hitting me?
Because it means promotion—another three blows and I'll be a sergeant and you'll be unconscious.

ison doctor's measurements of McGonagall

IGHT*	2 stone 11lbs with clothes (clothing on its own 2 stone 11)
IGHT	NIL Argyll United 3
FT LEG	23"
GHT LEG	4"
IST	16"
CK	6¼" (including shoulders)
AD	16 by 10 by 11 by 13 by 12 by 16¾
EST	unexpanded 16, expanded 16.0000000000001
NDITION OF TEETH	– away on holiday
IR	Sandy
ES	16"
ION	Poor, but can locate threepenny bit at range of 6 miles
ARING	Poor, but can tell value of coin dropped at range of 4 mls.
ET	Yes. Size varying, throbbing between size 7 and 12

I hereby swear that the above measurements are correct in every detail and bear no relation to the man I was examining.

Signed

Dr Crippen MD Prison Doctor retd.

My Dear Mother, I'm writing to tell you that nothing is worn under the kilt —it's all in working order!
oooo - beautiful City of Glasgow.
What do you mean I'll go blind if I don't stop it —and where's it gone?
"Here I am daddy"

WALLS HAVE EARS AND FISTS AND ICES!

Hair today —gone tomorrow

That's for nothing —now look out!

Och! this mon boxes claiver!

The following conversation was recorded by a warder outside the cell containing McGonagall and the nude Bonnie Mary.

McGonagall: Hello there Jock.

Nude Mary: That's nae bludey gude to me.

McGonagall: You're a good looking fellow, where's your claes?

Nude Mary: Ah that's more like it.

McGonagall: I see ye've had it shot away then?

Nude Mary: Nae really. I find you short on experience.

McGonagall: I think we could be friends Jock.

Nude Mary: Well have it yor ain way, but as far as I'm concerned ye're missing the chance of a lifetime.

McGonagall: Och ye're an amusing laddie with a unique turn of phrase. I see ye've been wearing the sporran under the kilt.

Nude Mary: Now ye're getting warmer. Ye're awfu' clever to have noticed that.

McGonagall: It's not commonly known that when I'm holding ma breath and contracting ma abdominals I can increase ma body temperature by three degrees.

Nude Mary: Och You're awfu' clever and a twit.

McGonagall: You're too kind Jock and a well-built fella to boot, but I warn ye that long hair of yours could get ye intae trouble.

Nude Mary: I think I'll give ye a wee treat and dae a naval hornpipe for ye.

(see gaoler's photograph)

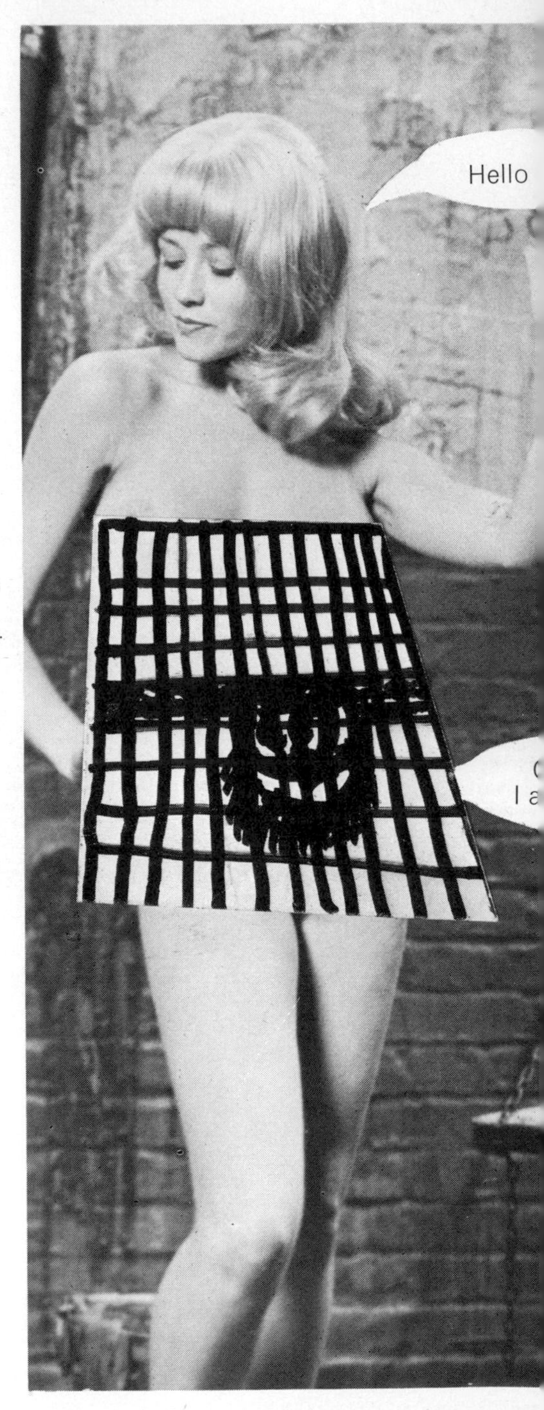

I'm no a sailor,
I'm a Scottish poet.
—And why did the
Mother Superior turn you in?
Och it all comes back to me
—NUDE NUN
IN NAUGHTY NIGHT
IN NEASDEN
PAKISTANI SHOCK
HORROR PROBE.
Phew what a scorcher
says Sun—A.P.
daddy

The merry hornpipe dance performed by the nude admiral Bonnie Mary which he enjoyed heartily and which caused McGonagall to interject frequently with cries of "Have ye any money or food", and inspired him to write the following lines.

Oh wondrous Admiral of the Fleet
Sae nifty and nimble on his feet
To see him dancing round the cell
Makes me feel extremely well
How lucky I am to be in Jail
With vigorous leaping done by a
powerful male
Who's powerful chest flew in all directions
At such a speed it defied all close inspections
But finally at midnight exhausted I
fell asleep
But he kicked me awake saying
'Get up you little creep'

The above poem was found in the deceased's effects. Among his effects were Motor Horn, Knock on Door, Bird Call, People Talking at Cocktail Party, Man Sawing Plank in Half, Feet Up Gravel Path, Charge of Cavalry at Waterloo, Jack The Ripper sharpening tools, Churchill Painting, and Mrs Ethel Teeth of Paddington.

RED HAIRY DAILY

Ed. Och MacKay sub ed. Admiral Doenitz

Today, taking advantage of the good weather, the Governor of McHairylegs Prison released McGonagall a full fourteen seconds before his time was up. Commenting on this generous gesture, McGonagall said "The milk of kindness has not dried up but Oh Christ it's in awful short supply".

So as not to embarrass the prison staff McGonagall was let out the back door with a blanket over his head and a boot up the back. He took with him his entire worldly posessions – an empty cardboard box, even that had a 'for sale' sign on it, and had been given to him by the nude admiral, who had kept her clothes in it.

He had a twenty mile walk ahead of him. Arriving at his home in a thunderstorm at midnight he was greeted by his wife who said: "Who are you?", to which he replied "I'm your husband, who are you?" and she replied "I am your wife, who are they?" and he replied "They are our children" and they replied "Who are we?", and McGonagall replied "We are your parents". It was a soul searching moment but the whole problem was cleared up when our reporter suggested that McGonagall removed the blanket from his head, whereupon the wife said "You are my husband, who am I?". "You are the mother of those children who happen to be mine" said McGonagall. This completed the roundelay. The policeman moved the crowd on and the McGonagalls in.

Our reporter then advised McGonagall that the police were taking no action. McGonagall found the house in a state of dilapidation. He called in an architect who he hit. "What's that for?" said the architect on his way down. "That was for you" said McGonagall. "See illustration on page . . ." said the architect. "Now get out" said McGonagall "see page . . . . ."

At which point our reporter left, believing himself to be an architect. B.U.P.

McGonagall telling his wife that he is her husband and vice versa.

McGonagall informing the architect that the floor was out of tr

MRS. JEAN McGONAGALL'S DIARY

That winter the McGonagalls starved

Our dear William came home from the prison today. The children and I knelt down and prayed that it would not be long before he would be back inside. I settled his rent at three shillings a week. We shall see. Many things needed doing to the house. Burning to the ground for instance. I've left matches all over the house but he does not take the hint. But he does take the matches and sells them to ME.

He says he cannae gae tae being an unemployed weaver full time. I asked him what he was now then and he replied "I am a full time unemployed dental mechanic aren't I?"

"I'd get more money than a weaver if I was employed" he said proudly, hanging in the window a notice saying 'WANTED BAD TEETH'.

"Och you're a silly mon' I said 'Why cant you be a full time unemployed millionaire like other men?"

"A good idea" he said, placing a notice in the window saying:

WANTED
MONEY
NO REASONABLE OFFER REFUSED

It was about this time that McGonagall decided to persist with becoming an actor, and he gave many recitals in Public Houses, Footpaths and Open Spaces.

His first professional appearance was at Wilton's Music Hall which was also his first paid appearance, that is he paid to appear.

His payment was so well received that they asked him to stay on for a further evening of misery for the audience.

On one such evening during a heavy fog, (property of the Church Commissioners), Queen Victoria lost her way to Wilton's Music Hall where she arrived safely just before McGonagall's futuristic impression of Max Miller, the green-bearded whistling yodeller from Penge.

It was love at first sight for McGonagall and he burst into an impromptu poem :-

'OOoooooooooooohhh jolly good Queen Victoria
How lucky you came into Wilton's tonight
I saw you sitting in the Royal Box
And I though 'That's nice'.

It was not one of his better poems but then none of them were.

At the end of his version of Macbeth, in which he rode a bicycle dressed as a Japanese Warrior, he thanked the audience for the magnificent vegetables they had 'bestowed' on him. "It's fine o ye tae pay in kind", he said. "Any kind is good enough for you mate" was the reply. That night high tide at Wapping Pier was at 8.20, as McGonagall found out. They threw him in it.

Signed - The Rev Gilfillan

Come in Max Miller No. 3 —your time is up.
I fell in love with Mary from the dairy (also Alice Crudge who when last seen was living at No. 13 Piles Road, Lewisham), But Mary didn't fall in love with me (nor did Alice Crudge of 13 Piles Road, Lewisham.)
This is one way of getting in free.

There must
be an easier way
to get rid of mice.
Sing it again Sam

Highlights of the dramatic descent of William

(Keep throwing the rotten vegetables – I'm hungry)

McGonagall

McGonagall acting the part of Shylock the Jew outside Sir Lew Grade's Kensington Mansion through lack of money.

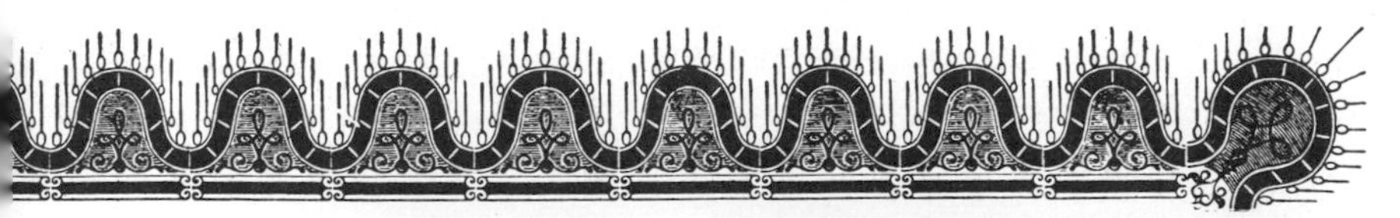

McGonagall's agent telling him there's nae work except for drag artistes.

McGonagall performing to a captive audience.

McGonagall meets Marty Feldman on an early L. P.

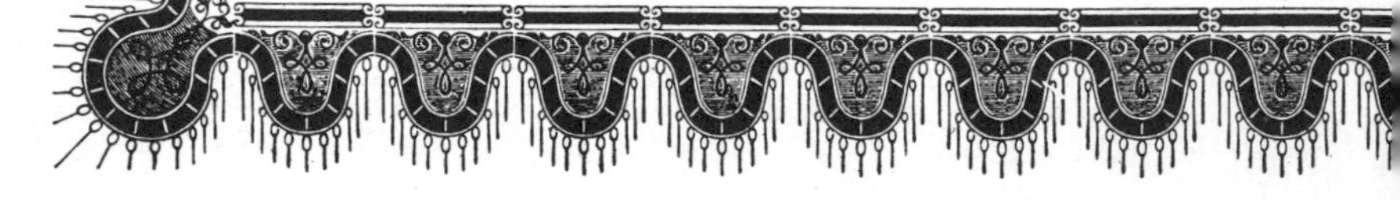

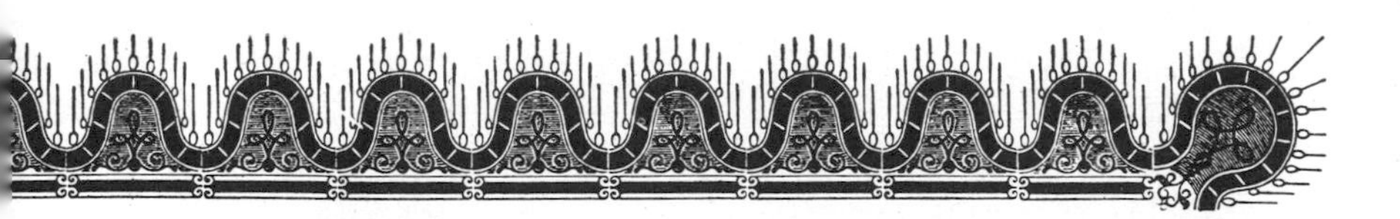

McGonagall in his youth teaching coloured ladies to play the violin through lack of money.

McGonagall departing to have tea with Her Majesty.

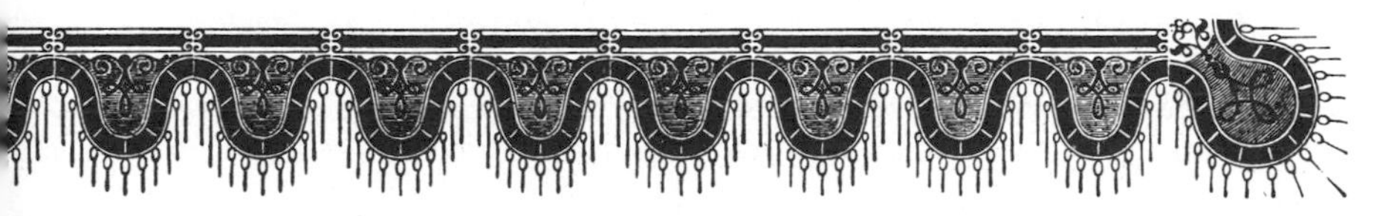

Exercises In Bed

A chart containing eighteen photographs of Bernarr Macfadden, reproducing a series of exercises which may be taken in bed, and which will bring gratifying results. The chart is handsomely printed in two colors, and is substantially mounted, and provided with hanger, so that it may be placed on wall of bedroom for convenience of those using it. Send for it to-day—you will be more than pleased with it. **Price, post free, 1s. 6d.**

A Child of Love

A Startling Story by Margaret Grant

The thrilling life history of a girl who comes into the world marked by the Bar Sinister of Love Out of Wedlock, and who makes a brave fight for existence without asking any favors from the world because of Her Sex.

PNEUMATIC

FACIAL MASSAGE ROLLER

The most perfect device ever invented for massaging face and neck.

No woman's toilet is complete without it. Assists in rounding out face and neck and fills in unsightly hollows around the collar bones. Device is made of spiral rubber rolls, soft and yielding to the flesh, bringing new blood to the parts far superior to hand massage. The most pleasant of all massage methods. You can actually feel the skin tingle as the new blood rushes in to replace the old when the soft rolls of rubber pass over it.

Price, 4s. 6d. Postpaid
Foreign Postage Extra.

Macfadden Physical Development

THE STRENUOUS LOVER

A Romance of Natural Love's Vast Power

By BERNARR MACFADDEN

An ideal gift for a young man or woma[n] If you cannot induce a young man or woma[n] to exercise and get strong, get them to rea[d] this inspiring book. Reading it will positivel[y] create a fondness for athletics which could n[ot] be done as well in any other way. This boo[k] contains 450 pages of the most valuable rea[d]ing matter. Beautifully bound in clot[h] sent postpaid. Regular Price, 4s. 10d. Fo[r]eign postage extra.

Fresh from his triumph at Wapping Pier and also his triumphal two week appearance at the Wapping Hospital Pneumonia ward, patrons will be glad to know that this favoured son of Wilton's has been re-engaged for an evening of audience projectile-hurling participation, during which your target will regale you with Shakespeare, melodies and soft-shoe shuffling (as

How To Prevent Constipation

An interesting and instructive pamphl[et] handsomely illustrated and with cov[er] printed in colors, matter by Berna[rr] Macfadden. It contains much usef[ul] information and how to prevent and cu[re] constipation, with illustrations and d[e]scriptions of the exercises adapted [to] treatment of this annoying complai[nt]

Macfadden's Physical Training

n illustrated system of exercise for the
velopment of health, strength and beauty,
y BERNARR MACFADDEN.

Contains ten full-page half-tone pictures of
e author in favorite classical poses. Instruc-
ons illustrated by full-page half-tone engrav-
gs. Price, in heavy paper binding, 1s. 2d.
oreign postage extra.

the hard ones are at the menders). Rotting vegetables will be on sale in the foyer free.

Patrons will be delighted to know that an equerry of Queen Victoria has requested that McGonagall attend Balmoral Castle for tea with Her Majesty.

signed Eric Giles
Fords of Dagenham

THE VACCINATION SUPERSTITION

his Book Contains an Article by Bernarr Macfadden on Vaccination

n essay on the impotency of vaccination as a
reventive of smallpox, by Dr. Hodge; an
ccount of Dr. Rodermund's experiment to
rove smallpox non-contagious; and Dr.
everson's famous table showing fatal simil-
ity between symptons of syphillis and the
sults of vaccination. Price 6d. Foreign
ostage extra.

Whitely Grip Machine

Strengthens the Wrists; Strengthens Fingers. Cures Writers' Cramps. Invaluable to Pianists and Writers.

One pair sent free for 3s. Foreign postage extra.

FREE TO THE RUPTURED

We will send free to anyone who is ruptured, a free trial of our famous home cure. It is a marvelous method, curing cases that defied hospitals, doctors, trusses, electricity and all else. Merely send your name and address on the coupon, and the free trial will be sent without any cost to you whatever. Mr. R. Wharton, 52 Domestic Street, Holbeck, Leeds, was ruptured 7 years. He tried this method, and has worn no truss for over 6 years; Mr. G. Thomas, 1 Station Road, Llansamlet, Glams., was ruptured 40 years. Has now worn no truss in 6 years. Mr. W. Lockwood, Tanton, Downham, Brandon, Suffolk, ruptured 30 years, not worn truss for 5 years. These men were cured by the Rice Method. Send coupon for full particulars.

R. WHARTON.

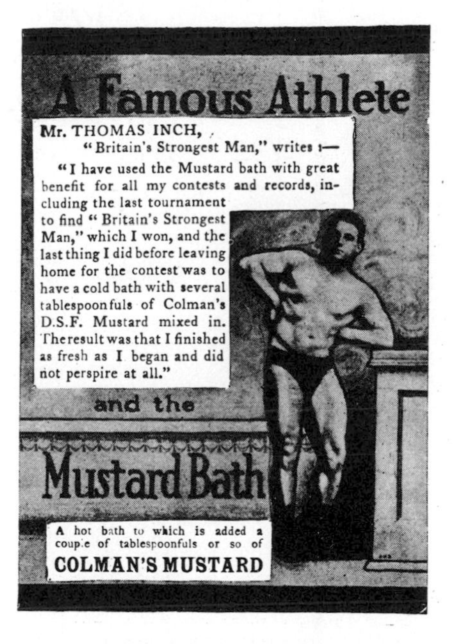

The Mystical Writings of the Rev Gilfillan, Vicar and Lunat
found under his Mattress at the Home for Insane Vicars.

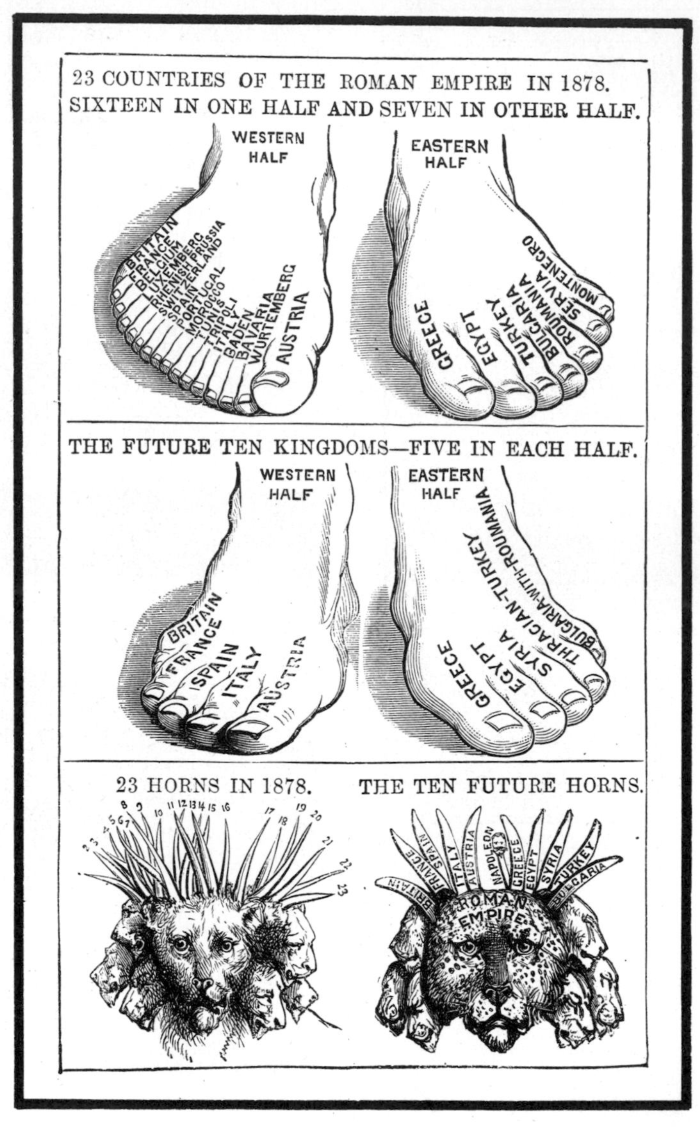

It was these documents that were instrumental in having him committed.

The ooft- of September 1890

Ma dear Wiff, mother tae my bairs, friend, confident +Co Ltd
with Branches in Grockie Street, also
estimates on pyro-nasal extinguishers Well, Im on ma
wee tae see ~~the~~ Her May the Quin, I have had fuve
terrible sexual experiences, 1, 2, 3, 4, 5 - Number 3 was
worst as the windows were closed. I have bin
given a room with running water through
the ceiling and permission to drink as much
as I like, and this goes for the air. I am
burning the midnight oil, ~~and~~ so I can see to
write a poem for it

Oooo oooooo beautiful midnight oil
Let nothing yew despoil
Ye are brighter than a candle
A less messy to handle
At one penny per quart
A considerable amount can be bought
And it casts a wonderful glow
Ying tong iddle I po.

At this point there came into ma room
a mon wearing a bowler hat and carrying a
brown paper parcel, he pushed past me intae
ma room, moved the furniture against the
wa's, tak off his claes and donned a pair of

spotted leotards stamped Glasgow Boro Council, "Best of three falls" he said and lunged at ma throat. For ten hours we grappled in the room, the battle going first one way and then the other both to his advantage. I, personally had never been tied in a granny knot before, but theres always a first time. then there was a second, third, fourth fifth and sixth time, In the end I coued resist the temptation nae linger 'Who are ye" I said my voice coming frae behind his buttocks, which was where I was at the tim, "I am Len Philatnackers, district visiting Wrestler, who are you"? I told him I was a Granny knot 6 times over", he then said "6 first falls to me sign here here here here here here and here, initial this and then sign it", "Signing taks a long time" I said; "Aye" he said "Its a sign of the times", I am also a "District visiting Joker" he added.

Your ever loving Laureat

William Macgonegal

Police Document on the whereabouts of William McGonagall

He's in Dundee.

signed: Inspector Thadeus MacFugget-NacFugget
Rabbi Extraordinary to the
Glasgow Police Choir

NOTE: McGonagall found the above report very useful in discoveri
his whereabouts which as you all know are not worn under the ki

Scrackaloogie Gazette

Sudnay the third October 1850

It was reported that William McGonagall, Pxxx,xxxxxdxxhx Pot and Tradegian pissed this way onroot to Balmoral Castle to have tea with the Quinn.¾ The whole village turned out its rubbish to throw at him on his cheery way. He waved cheerily as rocks bounced off his skill, but he took it all in good part and fainted.¾¾¾

He was given a night's lodgings at the police station provided he did his act through the½keyholes of prisoners cells as a punishment. The break out was not discovered till the morning. It took a cunning locksmithsss to uncouple McGonagall from the keyhole in the cell door which xxdxxxxxx was occupied by Bonnie Mary of Argyll¾who was once again performing her hornpipe, this time with devastating results,½ especially on McGonagall who was no longer fooleds by her Admiral disguised. and was heard to mintion "GxKxx OOOOOOOO hhhhh Will ye no luke at those Knockerrrs¾?"

"Yes I will xxxkxxxxxx no look at them" said a pious policeman placing the xx binoculars to the back of his head, at the same time clenching an aspirin between the knees. "You never know" he said "Headaches can strike anywhere these days, at which moment McGonagall was struck by a headache in the shin. "This is all ne to me" said McGonagall and pointedgNxxx to a ferrous metal cart wheel covered in turqiose plastic prunes some going by the name of David Conyers, decked with Lyrebird feathers and an occasional view of the sea all in the shape of seven headed leopard with cour tries written on its flank, going b the name of Napoleon. "I thi it's new to all of us" said t policeman through his bino lars. "Why are you talk through the back of your nec said McGonagall. "It's the way to get ¾ promotion" saic ¾ Ploliceman.

COMPOSITOR WANT
signec

LETTER FROM THE REVEREND GILFILLAN TO MISS MURIEL BODY, CHORISTER, ORGANIST AND SCREW.

My dear Miss Body.

Have you heard the wonderful news? William MacGonagall has been invited by the Quinn to 'tak' tea wi' her in her chamber at Balmoral. Apparently he is to make the journey on foot. Which one he has not yet decided.

He has prepared several brilliant gems of Celtic verse for the Quinn - Here is one of them.

'Oooooooh beautiful Your Majesty the Queen
You're the finest Queen that I've ever seen
I'm told that you're a very fine mother
And you're very tolerant of Prince Albert's brother
They say he has some unsavoury Teutonic habits
And does very strange things with ducks and rabbits
But dinnae worry Quinn sae fair
Although I'm writing this here I'll soon be there'

I ask you Miss Body. Have you ever heard anything sae dreadful? I fear for his life. Let us hope that the Quinn and her German husband have a good sense of humour and a bad aim. For at this very moment they say

Willie is twenty miles into his journey and going over the back of Ben Nevis, who was bending down at the time and they say he'll never play the piano again.

Fortimately for our dear William the Palace Guard is fully occupied trying to rid Balmorel of the Squon of Onnie, the Mugg of Arloo, the Nak of Quodge, the Quak of Thoo, the Sneg of Odge and, a late-comer, the Thudd of Borly. (Mrs. Bovingdon is still on holiday). The Scream of Agoni is expected later today. There are a total of six hundred and eighty three of these Eastern Potentates swarming all over Balmoral. As fast as they are pushed out the front door they come chattering in the back. The Pronce Cinsort has had the hoses on them for the last three days but the colour won't come off except for Mrs. Bovingdon who is on holiday. It is not a happy place, the Palace, which is perhaps why he has been invited there. It is my confirmed belief that he will be asked by the Quinn to recite poems at the Squons, Muggs, Naks, Quaks, Thudds and Snegs, and if he can't get rid of them Miss Body, then we must get married in the Spring and give the Queen a home.

Your ever loving wrinkled retainer

The Reverend George Gilffilan.

Rev. Gilfillan in an unguarded moment at the top of the Eiffel Tower.
photo taken by a Mrs. Horrible.

Weather Report in Balmoral Area

The Royal Weather broke at Balmoral where it snowed some 3 ft. deep on the slopes of Miss Muriel Body. All traffic has been stopped. No transport is running but McGonagall is still walking. A reporter for the Northern Blow, Mr. Bazoliken-Squitz (Mrs Bovingdon is on holiday), interviewed McGonagall in a deep snow drift. The conversation went thus:–

Squits. "Hallo? Is anybody down there?"

I never knew you could get dandruff as bad as this.
I say I say how can you avoid falling hair?
WILLIAM McGONAGALL and his POETIC GEMS TOURING SUIT CASE
Jump out of the way.

Dearie dearie Oh Oh Oh
Buried alive in the snow oh oh
Shiver shiver shiver sneeze
Look at the icicles on ma knees
Not only ma knees
But also ma rides
Oh where does it come from
And where does it gaes ?

The Alpine Brigade looking for McGonagall.

BUP Report

Extract from Northern Blow

Owing to the lack of response from the deep hole in the snow Mr Squits the Alpine Correspondent for the Northern Blow reported Gaelic groaning and shivering from a depth of 30 feet. He had reason to believe that somebody in distress was below the snow line. A rope was lowered down and pulled up with nothing on it. It was William McGonagall.

"My God" said the frozen McGonagall, "you have saved my life". "Oh no we haven't" responded a jolly fireman and sliced through the rope whereupon Mr. McGonagall was seen to descend again to the greater depth of 75 feet. "What in God's name did ye dee that for?" said McGonagall. "We were called out under false pretences, this is not a fire it is a snow drift. What you need is the snow brigade and you'll be hearing from our solicitors in the morning."

"Thank you" said McGonagall "There's nothing like getting a precise piece of technical information, I'll apply immediately through the normal channels for the snow brigade to save my life. Now will you please lower the rope". The fireman complied and McGonagall ate it.

"That's much better" said McGonagall "I feel much better for your fireman's rope. It will sustain me till the snow brigade arrives".

Further weather report from Balmoral Area
Freak weather shock horror. "91° Phew what a scorcher" says Private Eye headline. Today the hot sun brought floods of water some 30 ft deep. The Snow Brigade Alpine Rescue Team had fought its way through the water to rescue one William McGonagall who had reported that he was buried and suffering from snow blindness. Our reporter heard the leader say "You are a charlatan there's no snow or Alps here. If you have snow blindness why are you shouting 'Help I'm drowning'." "There's been a change of plan" was the reply. "What you need is a lifeboat, and you'll be hearing from our solicitors in the morning (Mrs Bovingdon is on holiday)" said the Alpine Snow Brigade.

The skipper of the lifeboat singing hymns rather than go out to rescue McGonagall.

The Wapping Life Boat setting out not to save McGonagall.

Mrs. Bovingdon on holiday watching McGonagall drown.

An action replay of McGonagall drowning.

Report from Sergeant Andrew Retch, Coldstream Guards,
Guard Commander, Balmoral Castle.

On the night of Friday the 6th October 1851 guardsman Tools reported heavy snow falling and asked permission to take refuge in the sentry box. However he was stopped by a wraith like figure who was sitting inside cooking a thin sausage over a match. Tools said "Here you wraith like figure put that light out, don't you know there's a war on?" Whereupon the wraith like figure answered, "What war and guardsman Tools replied "This one" and fired at his leg. But the bullet ricocheted off the sausage which was of a higher density than is usual. The bullet returned in the direction of guardsman Tools and entered the buttock just behind the bayonet scabbard. It then went in a northern trajectory entering the foot of the Squon of Onnie who was on the roof being chased by the Third Battalion. Whereupon guardsman Tool says "You naughty man. Look what you been and gorn and done?" and then screamed and fainted. Guardsman Tools having a big head we heard the thud from the guardroom. Corporal Sores said "Hello he's early tonight".

We apprehended the wraith who identified himself as one William McGonagall. He carried on his person a letter of introducti to the Quinn signed over a green shield stamp by Lt Fred Rollo of the Zulu War, South Africa.

Dear Quinn.

This is to introduce William McGonagall, Poet and Tragedian who wishes to give you a rendering of his works.

He's not the kind of man some
Would think of as handsome
But to my heart he carries the key

I can't explain
It's surely not his brain
That makes me thrill
I love him because -
There's nothing worn under the Kilt

Your loyal subject
Fred Rollo Lt.
Skinner's Light Horse
(The heavy one is away on holiday)

Court Circular Balmoral

May the Thing 1850

Today the Quinn received the Squon of Onnie and his retinue. He showed the Quinn his credentials and was immediately arrested by the Palace guard. The Quinn also received the American Ambassador Mr Hiram J Lootmildly IV. Later she received a blow on the head, the Squon of Onnie having escaped from the Palace guards.

There was a Royal Banquet in the grand Dining Hall originally intended for the Squon of Onnie, it was eventually eaten by the Mugg of Arloo who had not been received by the Quinn, but had been received by the American Ambassador who showed him the way to the dinner. He was court by the Caught Chamberlain or was he really caught by the Court Chamberlain. The Quinn dined alone with the Irish Guards on the food left over by the Squon of Onnie from another banquet which the American Ambassador had thrown for the Nak of Quodge in turn related to the Squon of Onnie. None of these was the relation of the Quak of Thoo who it was thought was in the Palace somewhere looking for the Smeg of Odge whose real name was Jim.

Mrs. Bovingdon is on holiday.

Royal Photo Album

Mr. Disraeli—I want a full report on what's worn under the kilt.

This day I have given audience to a man who was Scottish Artistic genius. He read me some of the nost exquisite poetry I have ever heard in my life vith the rich and powerful tones of his voice which ose and fell like the sea. Both Prince Albert and I were deeply moved by him But then he left and n came William McGonagall.

He presented me with a letter of introduction and vent into a poem which as I recall went something ike this.

Oooooohh Oooooooohhh Ooooooh Ooooooooooooh"

I thought at first this was the start of a poem but then I realised that he was holding his groin. Even then we were still puzzled for Albert turned to me and said "I think zat he iss von off der new action poets".

At this McGonagall bent down and pulled up his left sock and said

"Aaaaaaah that's better"

He then removed his shoe and emptied several rocks onto the flae saying

"There's some rocks on the flae"

"I'd rather they were there than in my shae"

He then raised his kilt revealing certain conditions and concluded with a couplet:-

"Ooooh powerful female leader of the British Raj

What time's tea your Maj?"

At this we withdrew into the tea parlour leaving him behind. We bolted the door but alas he came in through the window and with a wink, a nod, and a dig in the ribs of dear Albert he said

"Ye nae done sae bad for yersell for a Gerry-after all she could hae married John Brown or Guardsman Tool - she had the power tae choose!"

Harrods
—and hurry!

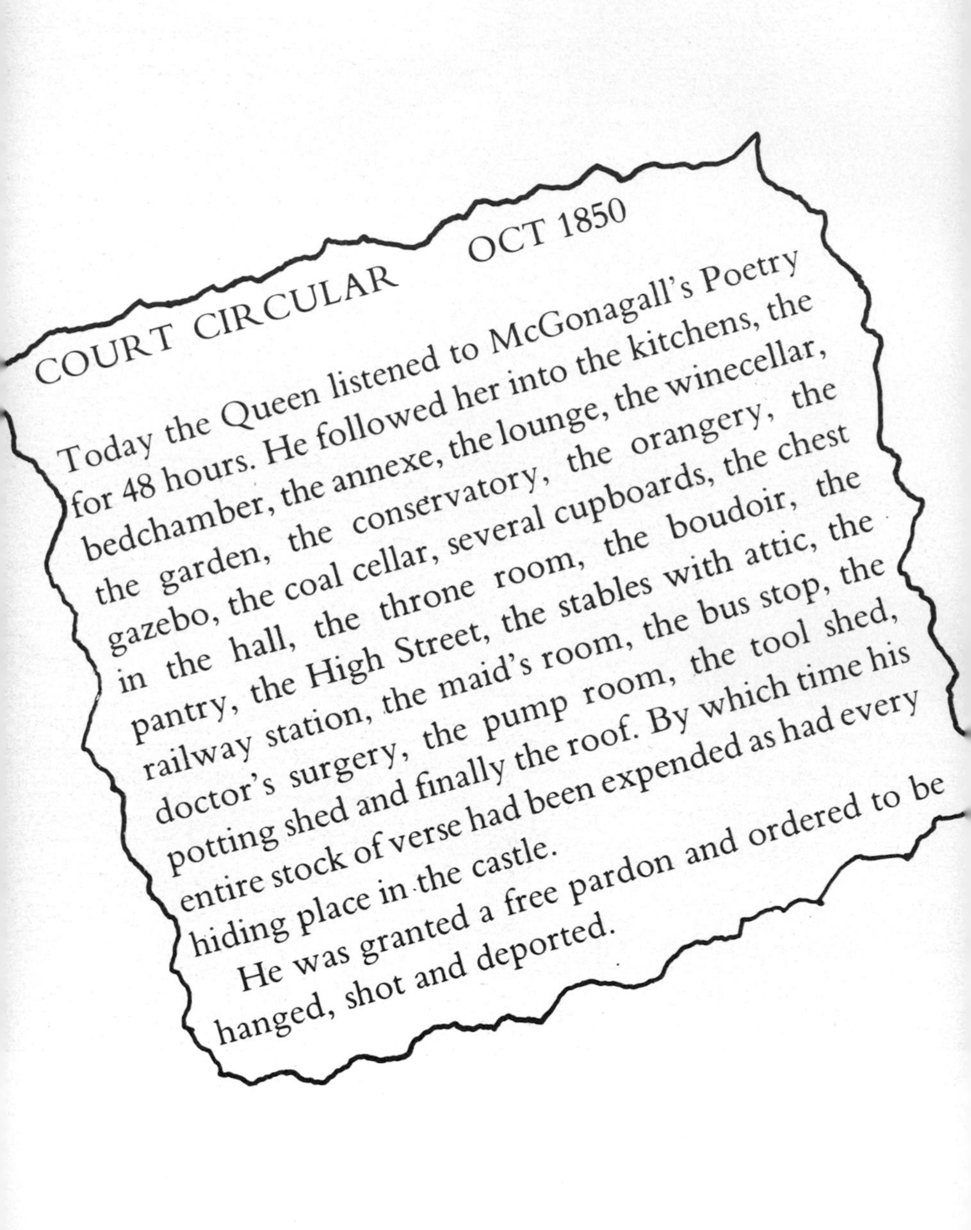

COURT CIRCULAR OCT 1850

Today the Queen listened to McGonagall's Poetry for 48 hours. He followed her into the kitchens, the bedchamber, the annexe, the lounge, the winecellar, the garden, the conservatory, the orangery, the gazebo, the coal cellar, several cupboards, the chest in the hall, the throne room, the boudoir, the pantry, the High Street, the stables with attic, the railway station, the maid's room, the bus stop, the doctor's surgery, the pump room, the tool shed, potting shed and finally the roof. By which time his entire stock of verse had been expended as had every hiding place in the castle.

He was granted a free pardon and ordered to be hanged, shot and deported.

When I apprehended him your honour he said, Yes I am head of the family.
My left arm is a sergeant.
Why put a zebra crossing here.
down here mummy.
Yes I did and Yes it is

McGonegall at the hitting section.

From the desk of Colonel Adolf Rabies

Commandant, Devil's Island (Hitting Section)

To the Mr. Louis Napoleon

Dear Emperor,

This is to advise you of le situation sur the Island. We 'ave recently 'ad une Homme Scots delivered free from Her Majesty Queen Victoria. I 'ave 'ad a look at 'im and zis could mean War. He says 'e is zer Poet Laureate de Angleterre but I suspect somezing. He speaks wiz zer accent Escossee and there iz pas de choses under the kilt - Tous marches perfectement - We await your instructions.

Adolf Rabies.

Signed - Adolf Rabies

Commandant

William MacGonegal
c/o Devils Island

Yeore Majesty the Quin,

What did i dee wrang? I faithfully followed ye thrae Balmoral Castle lightening your day with unending streams of powerful Scottish poetry which springs from deep doon in the roots of ma kilt. It was nay easy fra me to stay awake all nicht shouting ma poetry doon yer ear trumpet and up the bed claes, how do ye think I felt having tae climb up the roof after you [illegible] at the same time reciting Beautiful Bridge of the Silvery Tay, while yer husband fired at me with a shotgun. It was nae easy to recite 'The Sinking of the Collingwood' hanging from the gutter while Prince Albert jumped on ma fingers. I must also object at being sewn up in a coal sack and thrown in the moat, which was empty. However, I am nat familiar with the Royal ways, but as Poetry Sgt; Ulcers "You're a lucky man that was your initiation ceremony for the Laureateship", and he put me on a laureate-ship and thats why Im here. Thank you

Signed William MacGonegal
Poet Laureate
Devils Island

PS Will you ask the French to stop hitting me.

Paris Soir

SENSATION! LE SCOTTISCHE POET LAUREATE AVE DONE LE BUNK IN TEMPERATURE OF 80%

Phew quelle whata scorcher – says Yeuz Prive

THE TIMES

Hubert Scrotal, our man on Devil's Island, reports:

Reports are coming in from London that a mon has ecsaped from Devil' Island in a kilt. It was in the hitting yard when warders were relaxing from their labours at lunchtime that it was discovered one of the best loved convicts was missing from his screaming cage. "We will all miss his merry screams" said his gaoler Pierre Le Frogs.

"There's nothing we like better than a nice day's hitting, but now "he shook his head sadly "we'll have to go back to Dreyfus again" "We don't like doing that, it makes people say we're anti-semitic whereas we are quite ordinary lovable sadists".

The story goes that McGonagall, by thrusting a red hot needle into the sole of his foot, managed to leap the eighty foot wall in one bound. Waiting the other side of it was the Indian Ocean and seventeen sharks. But by inflating his kilt and performing certain functions he jettisoned himself towards the setting sun. He was last reported sailing up the Forth of Firth screaming "Sharks, sharks".

FIRTH OF FORTH WEEKLY

MAN WITH CHEWED LEGS DRAGGED ASHORE IN OLD FISHERMAN'S NET

"It's the best catch I've had this year" said Old Salt Shankers Smith "I've never caught a Poet Laureate before. He'll fetch a good price at the market".

LETTER FROM THE REVEREND O'FALLON

Dear Muriel,

I've heard distressing news. Our Poet Laureate William MacGonagall is lying on a fishmonger's slab in Billingsgate crustacean Market. It's hard to see how a skilled fishmonger cannot tell the difference between a haddock and a Poet Laureate. I was hard put to it to raise the money to buy him at the going price, for white fish for the day, of sixpence a pound. I bid sevenpence a pound which I considered a fair price for freshly caught Poet Laureate. If you had seen the look of bliss on his face as I slid him off the slab into a barrel of salt. "May the Lord preserve you" he said, "and may the salt preserve you" I said. I took him home and I massaged his puir legs which were full of teeth marks, some of them his. "I got hungry too" he said. "It was the sharks or me. Do you know what saved my legs?"

"No" I said.

"Oh dear" he said "Now I'll never know."

What in fact did propel the sharks away from him was the following:–

1 grm. wintergreen oil
2 lbs. ground spinach and lentils
1 ladle lukewarm olive oil
2 oz. saffron paste
1 spoonful mollasses
pinch of sandalwood
2 fine oz ground linseed nuts
1 oz. paste of quinine
1 cwt. steel filings.
Dr. Collis's Cullodian Throat Mixture
1 copy King James' authorised version
of the Bible
1 lb. Gallaghers Cut Black Shag

"Aye" said McGonagall "If it hadnt been for a' that the sharks would have had ma legs and parts adjacent."

Yours sincerely,
The Reverend George Gilfillan

P.S. Keep sending the money.

Desk Sergeant Tigernuts report on incident at the Fox and Vixen Whitechapel Lane

WHITECHAPEL POLICE STATION

Constable Railings was called to the above named pub by the Proprietor Herbert Snots. Apparently a Scotsman wearing a kilt smelling of fish asked for a drink of brandy to restore his faith in mankind, and instantly collapsed on the floor. The Proprietor Mr. Elliot said to the man "There's no alcohol sold in this pub we're all Jehova's Witnesses," whereupon the Scotsman collapsed for a second time and refused to get up. The police were called by the Proprietor Mr. Elveston. Constable Railings arrived and the Proprietor Mr. D'Alvarez said "This man refuses to stop being unconscious on the floor of my bar and is ruining our best wall to wall saw-dust." "Come on Scottish Man" said the constibule "This is no place for an alcoholic like you, this is a tee-totaller's pub and the constable accompanied him to 'THE RAGGED ARSE' where not only was he given a glass of brandy but the bottle was thrown at him as well. "I'll repay you in kind" said the Scottish man. He struck a dramatic poetry-pose, and took out from under his kilt a thin screed and started to read.

"OOoooooooooooooooh"

"Look out it's McGonagall" said somebody, "he's going to poetry".

In one second the bar was empty.

"Cor look what you been gorn and done" said the incensed Landlord, "You'll pay for this," and held out a large bowler hat size 7¾ and McGonagall filled it to the brim. "Just in time" he said.

"Stop" said the policeman. "This crime has gone far enough - this man is unfit for work; I wish to be taken off the case."

"OOoooooooooooooooh" commenced McGonagall again,

Looks to me like you've been sleeping under a cow.
I'm not opening this bottle till they've both gone.
It's a home made Ambre Solaire
Oh God I'm going to be in here all night Daddy..

"Oooooooooooooh brave constable of London Town
With fine blue eyes and teeth of brown
The crime figures go up and then come down
But ye go on for aye.
Ting aling aling long ding dong ding
Listen I can hear the welkin ring
Roll up your truncheon and start tae sing
And ye can go on for aye
And ye brave barman with brandy and glass
The day will surely come tae pass
When ye're under the sod and covered with grass
And ye'll no gae on for aye.

Whitechapel Bugle

Fighting broke out late last night at the RAGGED ARSE, the society pub in Whitechapel, between a policeman, a poet and the proprietor Mr. Bing Crosby. Blows were exchanged. The Scottish Poet was rendered unconscious by the policeman, and was revived by the publican who was immediately rendered unconscious by the Scotsman, and was in turn revived by the policeman who was immediately rendered unconscious by the publican and revived by the poet.

At the inquest it was discovered that the Scotsman was still alive thanks to
1 grm wintergreen oil
2 lbs ground spinach and lentils
1 ladle lukewarm olive oil
2 oz saffron paste
1 spoonful molasses
pinch of sandalwood
2 fine oz ground linseed nuts
1 oz paste of quinine
1 cwt steel filings
Dr Collis's Cullodian Throat Mixture
1 copy King James's Authorised Version of the Bible
1 lb Gallagher's Cut Black Shag
and so the post mortem was adjourned until conditions became more favourable i.e. death.

To make recompense for the injustice, and to ensure that the next inquest was not wasted, he was booked to appear at THE RAGGED ARSE on what was laughingly called ASSASSIN NIGHT.

McGonagall
Live
at the
Ragged
Arse

Tartan Records

'he following is a notebook entry made
y the Drama Critic of the New York Herald
'ribune who attended this first night
remiere of McGONAGALL LIVE AT THE
:AGGED ARSE:* The Act apparently went
s follows:–

' Good evening ladies and gentlemen,
for my first item - Aaaaaaaagghhh -
Chrrrrrristtttt - Who threw that itaaaaaaaghh
for God's sake - CRASH - AAAAAaaaggh - stop
- aaagh Oh God - SPLAT ! "

There was then tab music as the body of the
actor was carried off stage and the curtains closed.
I think his act continued off stage. I could
not get the gist of it but it went something like
" SOMEONE CALL A DOCTOR ! "

All in all it was a unique performance of
great originality. It was amazing how he never
et one of the missiles miss him. He was always
n the right place at the right time. And how
e managed to meet that last great marrow face
n was a masterpiece of timing which nearly
ost him his life. How he can go on night after
night like this is beyond a humble American
critic's understanding, but he must be worth
every penny he gets which according to his
manager is somewhere in the region of
3½d to 4d a performance.

VARIETY

McGonagall retained second week at Ragged Arse

Audience slays artiste

"I'll come again and again until he's dead" said Gallery first nighter. Rehearsing in his hospital bed McGonagall said today "It's the big time for me"

"You can't get in" says the landlord

"I wish I couldn't" said McGonagall

"Is it going to be a long run?" says theatregoer

"Yes" says McGonagall breaking free and streaking for the hills.

His place has been taken by Bob Monkhouse.

From the Hills

Dear Jennie dear,

I ha bin a triumph at the The RAGGED ARSE for over one minute twenty (20) seconds, then, its Funne hoo a fickle populace gae teered o' there ~~the~~ Idol. I am sending you a bokay of ~~[illegible]~~ vegatables, all bruised but none ~~[illegible]~~ sae bad a me. I'll be setting oot fra' hame sune. How are the bairns, and the children? Is the muckle reek still on the drae? I'll wash it off when I come hame. Do the crummochs come oot on the griddle in the gloamings, if they do, shoot them. Remember ~~my~~ ma dear, there many a griggle before the dillock crickle wees the doodle. I forgot to tell ye. Im now a Poet Laureate, but dinna tell our creditors

Your Loving Laureate

Willie

S There nay glae in the grollic ma dear

McGonegal Personal Diary the 20th November 1883

Ooooooooh Diary

Up here in the rocky crags of Glen Teeth I have had time to think over my career and I reelise I haven't had one. All I need is one lift up a rung of the ladder of fame. Who'll gie it tae me? Today I met an old woman gathering sticks. It took me an hour to get her to let go of ma legs. which have never been the same since the Shark's ~~teth teat~~ teeth affair. On windy nights the wind blows through the holes and keeps me awake. But dinnae worry I'll have them plugged by the time I get hame to ma wife Jeannie and the bairns. Why should they have to suffer from the noise from ma legs?

I'm setting off today and I'm taking the following things.

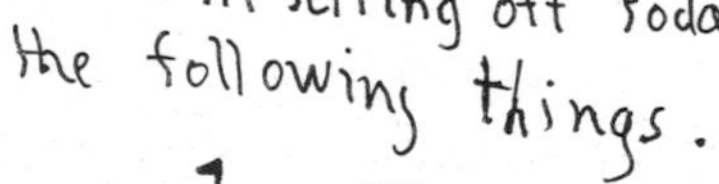

1. Me.

Highlights of the dramatic descent of William

(Keep throwing the rotten vegetables
– I'm hungry)

McGonagall

McGonagall trying to recover from the lack of money.

I'm sorry old boy
I'm not feeling for money
my braces have gone!

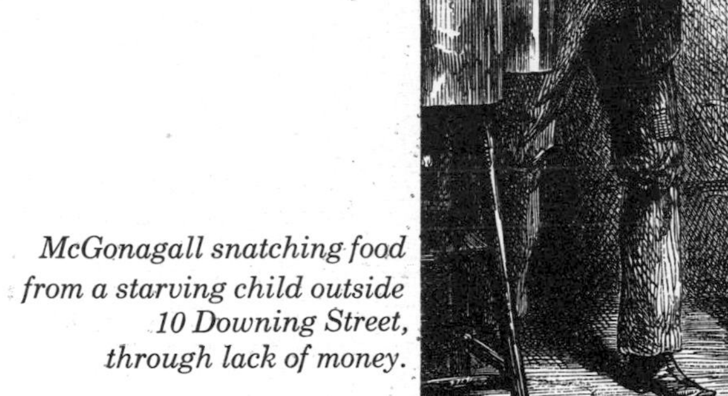

McGonagall snatching food from a starving child outside 10 Downing Street, through lack of money.

McGonagall being forced off the stage through lack of money.

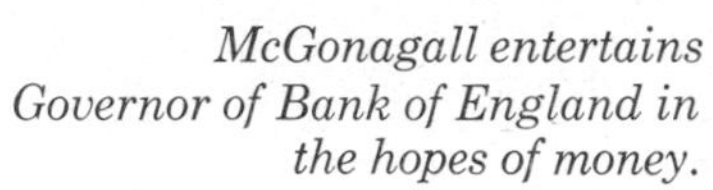

McGonagall entertains Governor of Bank of England in the hopes of money.

McGonagall forcing his act on an unsuspecting woman shopper.

The Bank Manager revealing the state of McGonagall's account to his wife.

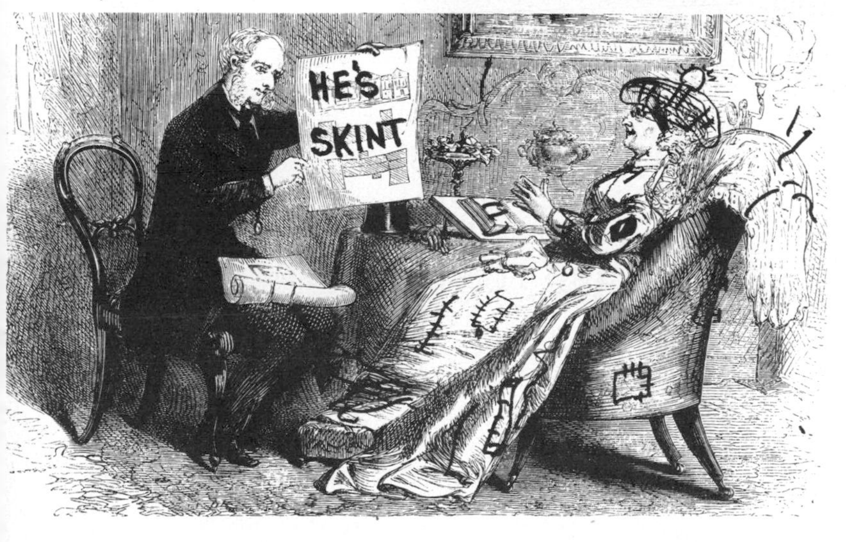

Congratulations! You've just won the United States in a raffle.
Signed President T-Type Ford.
Oh good that'll come in handy

Letter from The King Theebor of Burma

The Palace, Rangoon, Burma

Dear Mr. McGonagall,

I have seen some pictures of your poetry. They moved me very much in fact I haven't stopped going since I saw them and my physician wants the recipe.

I'm on my way to get it and if I see you you'll get it first. I'm coming with my entire retinue and a change of socks and three complete changes of Government.

You will soon recognise me because I will be carrying the order of the white elephant which I wish to bestow on you as I can't afford to feed it any longer. If either of you are not fond of elephants you have an alternative choice of a hundred year old parrot. There's only one trouble he's as big as an elephant. Mind you with massage and sauna baths, plastic surgery and extensive workouts he can be reduced in size to a different size. In any case that's all you're getting.

My retinue will be arriving at your home at 1600 hours Burmese summertime.

King Theebor

Signed - King Theebor

Emperor etc. the 3rd

Dear Muriel.

McGonagull is ill. So am I.

How are you?

Signed

The Reverend George Gilfillan

Padded cell

House for Insane Vicars

P.S. Excuse the writing but
it's not easy in a straight jacket.

William Gilfillan
the day before his death.
–Note the marked change in his appearance.

DAILY EXP

LORD BEAVERBROOK ANNOUNC
ENGLAND THROUGH THE ABBEY

Emperor etc 3rd Honours Scottish Gentleman Poet

Today at 23 Crappers Lane, Dundee a great treat was in store McGonagall family. "I was never so surprised in my life when th came to the door" said Mrs McGonagall. "He had a whole crowd of Poos with him, and I told him the nearest Curry restaurant was Street but the attendant said 'Dinnae mak a muckle on th noo b king and he can chop things off you so you'd better let him and his

The King was shown to the bedside of McGonagall. He didn't like the side so he got in. He quickly bestowed the order of the White Elephant and the aged parrot upon a speechless McGonagall who happened to be in bed with Lord Tennyson at the time as he was helping him with his deathbed speech which went,

Boldly they rode and well
Into the jaws of death
Into the mouth of hell
Rode the six hundred.

"That's a strange deathbed speech" said McGonagall. "Well you can modify it like this" said Tennyson

Boldly they rode and well
Into the jaws of death
Into the mouth of hell
Rode the six hundred.
But not McGonagall who was busy dying in Crappers Lane Dundee"

"OOOOoooooooh how silly of me to die
When there's nae sun in the sky . . . . ."
I do not wish to be put down
Unless my skin is nice and brown
Aaaaaaaargh aaaaaaaargh aaaaaargh . . . ."

"He's going . . . . ." said Tennyson "Can I have the bill please?". "There's nae bill" said Mrs McGonagall, "It's all free".

The phone rang. It was Queen Victoria. "I'm sorry you're dying" she said, "YOU'RE sorry", said McGonagall. "That's right", said the Queen "I'M sorry". "Well goodbye" she said.

"GOODBYE" said McGonagall and died.

There was a pause. "Reverse the charge" said the Queen.

"Very well" said T
"The reverse C Light Brigade" s son

"Ooooooh Bac
rode and we
Away from th
And I must sa
quite well .
Then he stop
"Mrs McGon
"Your husban
she said "Then
egg".

When W C
that McGona
Dundee he sa
comes of usin

THE PA
THREE H
THIRTY Y
MRS BOVI
ON

RESS

LANS TO BECOME QUEEN OF TIONAL

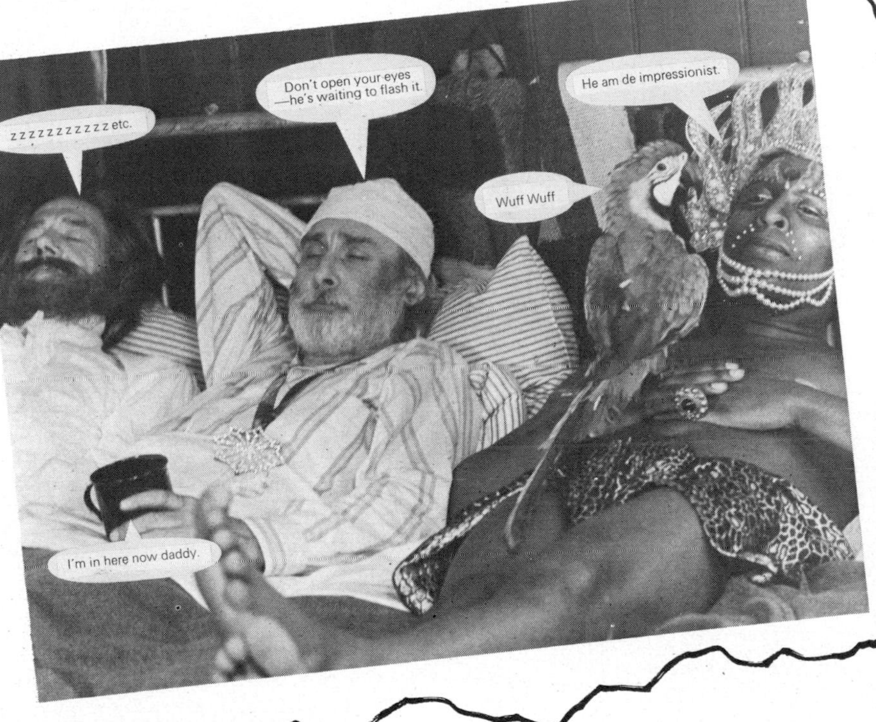

ne
ay-

y

nell
t

alled
'Oh''
l one

told
ed in
what
rial.''

OW
AND
) AND
, STILL

DYING CAN DAMAGE YOUR HEALTH
EVERY COFFIN CARRIES A GOVERNMENT HEALTH WARNING
Don't lower him down here
—this grave's full
—it's the time of year you kno

A selection of Poetic Gems by William McGonagall

THE RAILWAY BRIDGE OF THE SILVERY TAY

BEAUTIFUL Railway Bridge of the Silvery Tay!
With your numerous arches and pillars in so grand array,
And your central girders, which seem to the eye
To be almost towering to the sky.
The greatest wonder of the day,
And a great beautification to the River Tay,
Most beautiful to be seen,
Near by Dundee and the Magdalen Green.

Beautiful Railway Bridge of the Silvery Tay!
That has caused the Emperor of Brazil to leave
His home far away, *incognito* in his dress,
And view thee ere he passed along *en route* to Inverness.

Beautiful Railway Bridge of the Silvery Tay!
The longest of the present day
That has ever crossed o'er a tidal river stream,
Most gigantic to be seen,
Near by Dundee and the Magdalen Green.

Beautiful Railway Bridge of the Silvery Tay!
Which will cause great rejoicing on the opening day,
And hundreds of people will come from far away,
Also the Queen, most gorgeous to be seen,
Near by Dundee and the Magdalen Green.

Beautiful Railway Bridge of the Silvery Tay!
And prosperity to Provost Cox, who has given
Thirty thousand pounds and upwards away
In helping to erect the Bridge of the Tay,
Most handsome to be seen,
Near by Dundee and the Magdalen Green.

Beautiful Railway Bridge of the Silvery Tay!
I hope that God will protect all passengers
By night and by day,
And that no accident will befall them while crossing
The Bridge of the Silvery Tay,
For that would be most awful to be seen
Near by Dundee and the Magdalen Green.

Beautiful Railway Bridge of the Silvery Tay!
And prosperity to Messrs Bouche and Grothe,
The famous engineers of the present day,
Who have succeeded in erecting the Railway
Bridge of the Silvery Tay,
Which stands unequalled to be seen
Near by Dundee and the Magdalen Green.

THE TAY BRIDGE DISASTER

BEAUTIFUL Railway Bridge of the Silv'ry Tay!
Alas! I am very sorry to say
That ninety lives have been taken away
On the last Sabbath day of 1879,
Which will be remember'd for a very long time.

'Twas about seven o'clock at night,
And the wind it blew with all its might,
And the rain came pouring down,
And the dark clouds seem'd to frown,
And the Demon of the air seem'd to say—
"I'll blow down the Bridge of Tay."

When the train left Edinburgh
The passengers' hearts were light and felt no sorrow,
But Boreas blew a terrific gale,
Which made their hearts for to quail,
And many of the passengers with fear did say—
"I hope God will send us safe across the Bridge of Tay."

But when the train came near to Wormit Bay,
Boreas he did loud and angry bray,
And shook the central girders of the Bridge of Tay
On the last Sabbath day of 1879,
Which will be remember'd for a very long time.

So the train sped on with all its might,
And Bonnie Dundee soon hove in sight,
And the passengers' hearts felt light,
Thinking they would enjoy themselves on the New Year,
With their friends at home they lov'd most dear,
And wish them all a happy New Year.

So the train mov'd slowly along the Bridge of Tay,
Until it was about midway,
Then the central girders with a crash gave way,
And down went the train and passengers into the Tay!
The Storm Fiend did loudly bray,
Because ninety lives had been taken away,
On the last Sabbath day of 1879,
Which will be remember'd for a very long time.

As soon as the catastrophe came to be known
The alarm from mouth to mouth was blown,
And the cry rang out all o'er the town,
Good Heavens! the Tay Bridge is blown down,
And a passenger train from Edinburgh,
Which fill'd all the people's hearts with sorrow,
And made them for to turn pale,
Because none of the passengers were sav'd to tell the tale
How the disaster happen'd on the last Sabbath day of 1879,
Which will be remember'd for a very long time.

It must have been an awful sight,
To witness in the dusky moonlight,
While the Storm Fiend did laugh, and angry did bray,
Along the Railway Bridge of the Silv'ry Tay.
Oh! ill-fated Bridge of the Silv'ry Tay,
I must now conclude my lay
By telling the world fearlessly without the least dismay,
That your central girders would not have given way,
At least many sensible men do say,
Had they been supported on each side with buttresses,
At least many sensible men confesses,
For the stronger we our houses do build,
The less chance we have of being killed.

AN ADDRESS TO THE NEW TAY BRIDGE

BEAUTIFUL new railway bridge of the Silvery Tay,
With your strong brick piers and buttresses in so grand array,
And your thirteen central girders, which seem to my eye
Strong enough all windy storms to defy.
And as I gaze upon thee my heart feels gay,
Because thou are the greatest railway bridge of the present
day,
And can be seen for miles away
From north, south, east, or west of the Tay
On a beautiful and clear sunshiny day,
And ought to make the hearts of the "Mars" boys feel gay,
Because thine equal nowhere can be seen,
Only near by Dundee and the bonnie Magdalen Green.

Beautiful new railway bridge of the Silvery Tay,
With thy beautiful side-screens along your railway,
Which will be a great protection on a windy day,
So as the railway carriages won't be blown away,
And ought to cheer the hearts of the passengers night and day
As they are conveyed along thy beautiful railway,
And towering above the silvery Tay,
Spanning the beautiful river shore to shore
Upwards of two miles and more,
Which is most wonderful to be seen
Near by Dundee and the bonnie Magdalen Green.

Thy structure to my eye seems strong and grand,
And the workmanship most skilfully planned;
And I hope the designers, Messrs Barlow & Arrol, will
prosper for many a day
For erecting thee across the beautiful Tay.
And I think nobody need to have the least dismay
To cross o'er thee by night or by day,
Because thy strength is visible to be seen
Near by Dundee and the bonnie Magdalen Green.

Beautiful new railway bridge of the Silvery Tay,
I wish you success for many a year and a day,
And I hope thousands of people will come from far away,
Both high and low without delay,
From the north, south, east, and west,
Because as a railway bridge thou are the best;
Thou standest unequalled to be seen
Near by Dundee and the bonnie Magdalen Green.

And for beauty thou art most lovely to be seen
As the train crosses o'er thee with her cloud of steam;
And you look well, painted the colour of marone,
And to find thy equal there is none,
Which, without fear of contradiction, I venture to say,
Because you are the longest railway bridge of the present
    day
That now crosses o'er a tidal river stream,
And the most handsome to be seen
Near by Dundee and the bonnie Magdalen Green.

The New Yorkers boast about their Brooklyn Bridge,
But in comparison to thee it seems like a midge,
Because thou spannest the silvery Tay
A mile and more longer I venture to say;
Besides the railway carriages are pulled across by a rope,
Therefore Brooklyn Bridge cannot with thee cope;
And as you have been opened on the 20th day of June,
I hope Her Majesty Queen Victoria will visit thee very soon,
Because thou are worthy of a visit from Duke, Lord or Queen,
And strong and securely built, which is most worthy to be seen
Near by Dundee and the bonnie Magdalen Green.

THE RATTLING BOY FROM DUBLIN

I'M a rattling boy from Dublin town,
I courted a girl called Biddy Brown,
Her eyes they were as black as sloes,
She had black hair and an aquiline nose.

Chorus

Whack fal de da, fal de darelido,
Whack fal de da, fal de darelay,
Whack fal de da, fal de darelido,
Whack fal de da, fal de darelay.

One night I met her with another lad,
Says I, Biddy, I've caught you, by dad;
I never thought you were half so bad
As to be going about with another lad.

Chorus.

Says I, Biddy, this will never do,
For to-night you've prov'd to me untrue,
So do not make a hullaballoo,
For I will bid farewell to you.

Chorus.

Says Barney Magee, She is my lass,
And the man that says no, he is an ass,
So come away, and I'll give you a glass,
Och sure you can get another lass.

Chorus.

Says I, To the devil with your glass,
You have taken from me my darling lass,
And if you look angry, or offer to frown,
With my darling shillelah I'll knock you down.

Chorus.

Says Barney Magee unto me,
By the hokey I love Biddy Brown,
And before I'll give her up to thee,
One or both of us will go down.

Chorus.

So, with my darling shillelah, I gave him a whack,
Which left him lying on his back,
Saying, botheration to you and Biddy Brown,
For I'm the rattling boy from Dublin town.

Chorus.

So a policeman chanced to come up at the time,
And he asked of me the cause of the shine,
Says I, he threatened to knock me down
When I challenged him for walking with my Biddy Brown.

Chorus.

So the policeman took Barney Magee to jail,
Which made him shout and bewail
That ever he met with Biddy Brown,
The greatest deceiver in Dublin town.

Chorus.

So I bade farewell to Biddy Brown,
The greatest jilter in Dublin town,
Because she proved untrue to me,
And was going about with Barney Magee.

ATTEMPTED ASSASSINATION OF THE QUEEN

God prosper long our noble Queen,
  And long may she reign!
Maclean he tried to shoot her,
  But it was all in vain.

For God He turned the ball aside
  Maclean aimed at her head;
And he felt very angry
  Because he didn't shoot her dead.

There's a divinity that hedgeth a king,
  And so it does seem,
And my opinion is, it has hedged
  Our most gracious Queen.

Maclean must be a madman,
  Which is obvious to be seen,
Or else he wouldn't have tried to shoot
  Our most beloved Queen.

Victoria is a good Queen,
  Which all her subjects know,
And for that God has protected her
  From all her deadly foes.

She is noble and generous,
  Her subjects must confess;
There hasn't been her equal
  Since the days of good Queen Bess.

Long may she be spared to roam
  Among the bonnie Highland floral,
And spend many a happy day
  In the palace of Balmoral.

Because she is very kind
  To the old women there,
And allows them bread, tea, and sugar,
  And each one to get a share.

And when they know of her coming,
  Their hearts feel overjoy'd,
Because, in general, she finds work
  For men that's unemploy'd.

And she also gives the gipsies money
  While at Balmoral, I've been told,
And, mind ye, seldom silver,
  But very often gold.

I hope God will protect her
  By night and by day,
At home and abroad
  When she's far away.

May He be as a hedge around her,
  As He's been all along,
And let her live and die in peace
  Is the end of my song.

THE MOON

BEAUTIFUL Moon, with thy silvery light,
Thou seemest most charming to my sight;
As I gaze upon thee in the sky so high,
A tear of joy does moisten mine eye.

Beautiful Moon, with thy silvery light,
Thou cheerest the Esquimau in the night;
For thou lettest him see to harpoon the fish,
And with them he makes a dainty dish.

Beautiful Moon, with thy silvery light,
Thou cheerest the fox in the night,
And lettest him see to steal the grey goose away
Out of the farm-yard from a stack of hay.

Beautiful Moon, with thy silvery light,
Thou cheerest the farmer in the night,
And makest his heart beat high with delight
As he views his crops by the light in the night.

Beautiful Moon, with thy silvery light,
Thou cheerest the eagle in the night,
And lettest him see to devour his prey
And carry it to his nest away.

Beautiful Moon, with thy silvery light,
Thou cheerest the mariner in the night
As he paces the deck alone,
Thinking of his dear friends at home.

Beautiful Moon, with thy silvery light,
Thou cheerest the weary traveller in the night;
For thou lightest up the wayside around
To him when he is homeward bound.

Beautiful Moon, with thy silvery light,
Thou cheerest the lovers in the night
As they walk through the shady groves alone,
Making love to each other before they go home.

Beautiful Moon, with thy silvery light,
Thou cheerest the poacher in the night;
For thou lettest him see to set his snares
To catch the rabbits and the hares.

I earnestly hope the inhabitants of the beautiful city of Dundee
Will appreciate this little volume got up by me,
And when they read its pages, I hope it will fill their hearts with
delight,
While seated around the fireside on a cold winter's night;
And some of them, no doubt, will let a silent tear fall
In dear remembrance of

WILLIAM M'GONAGALL.